The Chorister and the Racing Car

A guide to high performance singing

Anita Morrison

with illustrations by Karen Fardell

Copyright © 2017 Anita Morrison All rights reserved.

No part of this book can be reproduced in any form or by written, electronic or mechanical, including photocopying, recording, or by any information retrieval system without written permission in writing by the author.

Published by Whole Self Singer

Printed by Book Printing UK www.bookprintinguk.com

Remus House, Coltsfoot Drive, Peterborough, PE2 9BF

Printed in Great Britain

First reprint

Although every precaution has been taken in the preparation of this book, the publisher and author assume no responsibility for errors or omissions. Neither is any liability assumed for damages resulting from the use of information contained herein.

Acknowledgements

Many thanks to Karen Fardell for her beautiful, witty illustrations, to her son Alfie for his contribution and to my husband, Bill, for his creative and humorous input. Also all of the choristers and choral directors I have worked with, particularly those at Westminster Cathedral on whom the book is based. They have played a major part in developing my teaching and given me such joy over the years, inspiring me to put this book together.

Contents

3	**Introduction**	
5	**Under the bonnet**	How your voice works
13	**General maintenance**	Vocal health
15	**Lubrication**	Hydration
17	**Ergonomics**	Physical alignment
22	**Servicing**	Stay fit and healthy
26	**Every day use**	Taking care of your voice
29	**Pit Stop**	First Aid
31	**Ready, steady, go!**	Warm up, rehearse, perform
33	**Pre-race routine**	The warm-up
34	**The practice run**	The rehearsal
35	**The big race**	The performance

Introduction

The voice is a very special instrument. Every single one is completely unique; no one else has a voice that sounds like yours. You use it to **speak** to your friends, **shout** for the ball on the sports pitch, express happiness, sadness, delight and anger, **whisper** your secrets, **cough** when you have a cold, and of course, for **singing**. It is with you 24 hours a day, 365 days a year for the whole of your life. You can't pack it away in a case like a violin or trumpet in order to stop it getting broken or dented, it is a living thing. You need to learn how to look after it so that it is in peak condition for top performance...

Think of your voice as though it's a high-performance racing car, about to take to the track in perfect running condition. The moving parts well oiled, the tyres well inflated, the tank filled with top quality fuel, the bodywork sleek and well maintained with victory in sight.

A neglected, rusty old banger might get you down to the shops but it's unlikely to get you to the chequered flag on the big day…

Under the bonnet

How your voice works

How your voice works

Inside your neck is the **larynx**. It is sometimes called the voice box and is where the sound is made. To find it, put your hand at the front of your neck and swallow. You will feel a little bump which moves up and down as you do so; this is your larynx. It will also go down when you yawn. When you make a sound you'll feel it make a buzzy vibration.

The larynx is a complex structure whose main function is to stop food entering the windpipe (**trachea**) and getting into your lungs by accident. It is made up of a number of parts which work together in the reflex actions of swallowing and coughing. You may have felt it trigger if you've breathed in a feather or choked on a piece of food because you've been talking while you were eating…

Stretched across your larynx from front to back are two small bands of muscle and tissue. These are called the **vocal folds** or **vocal cords**. They are joined together at the front but able to move at the back to open and close the gap between them.

The vocal folds are tiny, about 1cm long in children and can grow up to 2.5 cm long in an adult man. They close together when you swallow or cough and vibrate, creating a buzzing sound when air passes between them. This is just like when you blow up a balloon, pinch and stretch the neck out and make a squealing noise.

How do you think this works?

Try this experiment…

Hold up two pieces of paper with the thin edges facing you, about 5cm apart. If you blow gently between them what do you think will happen?

Will they flap around?

Will they move apart?

Will they do something else…?

What happened?

They get sucked together!

Were you surprised?

The scientist Bernoulli discovered this phenomenon and it is called the Bernoulli effect after him. Most people think that the pages will fly apart but they actually move towards one another.

As you sing, breath passes through the gap between the vocal folds. This gap is called the **glottis**. You may have heard the term 'glottal stop'.

Try this… say 'Uh Oh'. Can you feel how the vocal folds stop the breath by closing the gap?

When the air travels through the glottis, the vocal folds, which are very flexible, are sucked together by the air (the Bernoulli effect). Pressure builds up under the closed vocal folds and when the pressure below becomes greater than the pressure above, they open and the cycle repeats many times per second. This makes a buzzing sound which is the source of your voice.

A concert **A** is made up of 440 cycles of your vocal folds opening and closing every second.

A top **C** is 1046 cycles per second, imagine that!

Your vocal folds are apart at the back in silent breathing, clamp shut when you cough or swallow and positioned very close together when you speak or sing. As long as the breath is flowing, a sound can be made.

You have muscles inside your larynx that change the pitch. One set makes them longer and thinner and the pitch goes up, the other set shortens and thickens them and the pitch goes down. It's similar to twanging an elastic band; stretch it and the pitch goes up, relax it, the pitch goes down.

Once the sound is being produced, you can shape and change it using your tongue, lips, mouth and imagination.

Now you can get on and sing!!!

General maintenance

Vocal health

Lubrication – Hydration

Try this experiment…

Rub your hands together for a few seconds. What happens to them? Can you feel them getting hotter? If you kept going they would get red and eventually quite sore. This is caused by **friction**.

Now put some soap on your hands and try again. Can you feel how your hands slide easily and don't get hot? This is because of **lubrication**.

A car has lots of moving parts which need oil to lubricate them to reduce the friction that causes them to become hot, worn out or stuck when they rub together. To keep the car running smoothly the old, dirty, thick oil is regularly changed for new, clean, thin oil.

Your body doesn't work on oil but creates a substance called **mucus**. This mucus provides the lubrication for your voice, protecting the vocal folds from friction as they open and close many times a second. Too much friction will mean that the folds get tired quickly, and become swollen, making it much more difficult to sing. To make enough mucus to lubricate your vocal folds your body needs to be well hydrated. Doctors recommend at least 8 glasses of water every day.

You need to drink regularly, before you're thirsty, as it takes several hours for the water to be absorbed into your body. Once the water is absorbed it can produce the thin mucus needed to oil your voice.

Ergonomics – Physical alignment

You would never dream of driving your car with flat tyres, kinked or squashed hoses and ruined suspension. You might be able to limp to the garage but you'll never win a race.

You sing with your whole body, not just your larynx.

Does every part of you line up; ankles, knees, hip joints, shoulders, ears? If you drew a line between them, would it be straight?

When the line is straight we would call it good **physical alignment**.

It's a bit like creating a tower with building blocks

If the tower is wonky, the centre of gravity will be over to one side and cause it to topple over.

If you often stand with more of your weight on one leg than the other, you will be battling with gravity not to pull you over. The muscles which need to be available to help you to sing will be preoccupied with stopping you from falling over rather than being available to help you to sing well.

If you don't think about this, wonkiness can easily become a habit which is very difficult to get rid of.

If you build the tower straight, the centre of gravity will be in the middle and the force of gravity will pull down on the bricks, helping to keep it upright.

Make friends with gravity.

If your skeleton is lined up and your weight is evenly spread over both feet, then the muscles have very little extra work to do.

Your feet give a good base for the legs, your knees and hip joints can be loose, your arms can hang softly and your neck can be free, with your head balancing on the top.

You should be able to move anywhere from here without any preparation. Can you step to the right? Step to the left? Move forwards? Move backwards? Jump in the air? Touch the floor? Go for a walk?

The word **posture** is often used but implies something static, like a post. The way we balance ourselves is dynamic and always changing.

Try this experiment…

Stand and close your eyes. Can you feel all the little wobbles in your feet and ankles? These are caused by the muscles readjusting to keep you upright. The little movements are always present but we don't notice them when our eyes are open. The term physical alignment is more accurate, and we can carry this around with us all day.

If you're ready to move, then you're ready to sing!

21

Servicing – Stay fit and healthy

A racing car needs to be properly serviced, its moving parts in good repair and filled with premium quality high octane fuel in order to run at optimum efficiency.

Make sure you eat plenty of **healthy foods** including lots of fruit and vegetables to keep you strong and resistant to illness.

Get plenty of quality **sleep** to recharge your batteries.

Get plenty of **exercise** to keep you fit and physically strong.

BUT... Don't over use or abuse your voice by shouting harshly in the playground or on the sports field as it can put too much stress on your vocal folds and tire them out.

If you use "whooping" sounds or words with ee or oo vowels this will not be as tiring for your voice; for example "here" or "to me" rather than "mine".

Happy calling is much less tiring or damaging to your voice than angry or aggressive shouting.

Every day use – Taking care of your voice

Using your racing car every day is fine as long as you **look after it**. You just need to drive it well.

Don't grind the gears and don't rev up the engine unnecessarily. Don't overload it; you might damage the suspension, crack the chassis or blow a valve.

Never overload, force or abuse your voice.

The cracks will surely follow…

Drive appropriately for the conditions. If you drive too fast in the wet or take a corner in the wrong gear, you might skid off the track and have a nasty accident.

Always **use your voice appropriately** for the conditions. If someone is next to you, there is no need to speak loudly. If there is noise in the background, don't try to compete with it by raising your voice, go over to them in order to have a conversation.

Accident avoided...

Take heed of any warning lights or unusual bumps or grinding. You wouldn't dream of carrying on with a flat tyre or the oil light on, would you?

You should never carry on singing if it is uncomfortable or hurts as you can cause long-term damage.

If your voice is tired or husky, this is your warning. Rest your voice and rehydrate.

If your throat is sore, don't use anaesthetic throat lozenges or sprays as they mask the problem. This is like switching off the warning lights or turning up the radio so that you can't hear any bumping or grinding sounds.

If you are worried about your voice make sure you mention it to whoever is looking after you. Always ask for their advice.

Pit Stop – First aid

Every singer becomes ill from time to time.

Your voice will come back quickly if you take care of it. The best remedies for colds, sore throats and coughs are very simple, you rarely need strong medications.

If you just feel a bit gunky do your best to avoid repeatedly clearing your throat as this aggravates your vocal folds and causes them to form more mucus (remember **friction**) as they try to protect and lubricate themselves. It is better to swallow, sip water or gently puff out some air through open folds to knock any gunk off them.

Steaming – fill a big bowl with hot, steamy water (not boiling), lean over it with a towel over your head and breathe in the steam. You don't need to add anything. The steam helps thin mucus in your lungs, can ease coughing, lubricates your vocal folds and the warmth helps the muscles to relax.

Salt water gargle – dissolve some salt in warm water just enough to taste that it is there and gargle with it. This isn't very pleasant but it is the best way to treat a sore throat. Salt is an amazing antiseptic!

Make sure you spit it out. You don't want to swallow salty water.

Ready, steady, go!

Warm up, rehearse, perform

Pre-race routine – The warm-up

Pre-race, check the oil level, that the moving parts are sliding smoothly, there are no bumping or grinding noises, all the lights are working, mirrors adjusted correctly and the controls operating well. Warm up the engine and tyres and get ready for the race.

Make sure that you are well hydrated, your voice isn't sore or husky and you are fit and ready to sing. Take time to **warm up your body** first with some movement. Pay attention to your physical alignment; is the weight evenly distributed between both your feet, are your knees soft and the rest of you balancing over them? Is your jaw free? Is your tongue free and ready to articulate and express the words?

There are lots of ways to **warm up your voice** and your teacher or choir director will help you with this. One way to begin, is with the breath. Hiss out on a long 'ff', 'ss' or 'sh'. You can then add your voice so that the sound becomes a buzzy 'vv', 'zz' or 'zh'. You can also make sounds on lip trills/bubbles and tongue trills/rolled rs (with or without voice) or siren on an 'ng'. Start with a comfortable pitch and then slide around, gradually extending your range.

The Practice Run – The rehearsal

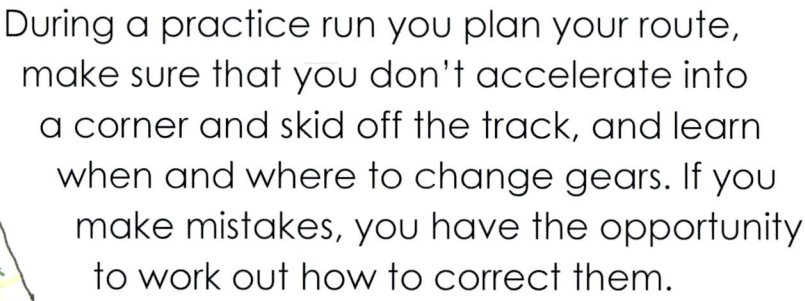

During a practice run you plan your route, make sure that you don't accelerate into a corner and skid off the track, and learn when and where to change gears. If you make mistakes, you have the opportunity to work out how to correct them.

In a choir rehearsal you learn the notes, how to pronounce the words and understand their meaning, how to shape the phrases, plan where to take the breaths and when to sing loudly and quietly. Don't be scared to make mistakes, but have courage to make new mistakes rather than the same one again and again.

The Big Race – The performance

Once you're really prepared you can take advantage of all your hard work.

By keeping your eyes on the road and staying focused you can have fun, be creative and enjoy the ride!!!!

Anita Morrison has taught singing to choristers and young singers for over twenty-five years including Westminster Cathedral, Temple Church, St George's Windsor Castle, Cardinal Vaughan Memorial School, The London Oratory School and Eton College. She has also taught at Cambridge University and the Guildhall School of Music and Drama in London. Having initially qualified as a primary school teacher Anita went on to study singing at the Guildhall School of Music and Drama and National Opera Studio and began teaching alongside her performing career. She has a deep interest in vocal health and good body use and qualified as a Feldenkrais Practitioner in 2015. In 2017 she was awarded an Honorary ARSCM in recognition for her work with choristers.

Karen Fardell is an architect and has been involved with Westminster Cathedral for several years as a chorister parent. She trained at Portsmouth School of Architecture and RWTH in Aachen. Her work includes extensive experience in re-use of historic buildings, their extension and repair. She currently lectures on a part time basis at Anglia Ruskin University on the Architecture courses. Along with her Architectural work Karen is a Printmaker; she has exhibited and sold through a number of galleries in East Anglia and London.